101
Uses
for a
CAT

101 Uses
for a
CAT

Edited by Andrea Donner

Willow Creek®
P R E S S

101 Uses for a Cat
Edited by Andrea Donner

Published by Willow Creek Press
P.O. Box 147 • Minocqua, Wisconsin 54548

For information on other Willow Creek titles, call 1-800-850-9453

Design: Pat Linder

Library of Congress Cataloging-in-Publication Data

101 uses for a cat / edited by Andrea Donner.
 p. cm.
 ISBN 1-57223-575-6 (hardcover : alk. paper)
 1. Cats--pictorial works. 2. Photography of cats. I. Title:
One hundred one uses for a cat. II. Title: One hundred and one
uses for a cat. III. Donner, Andrea K.
 SF446 .A155 2002
 636.8'0022'2--dc21
 2002001085

Printed in Canada

Cats as companions…

Someone to come home to

2

Someone to read bedtime stories to

3 Someone to picnic with

© Bonnie Nance

4 *Surrogate sister*

5 *Hand warmer*

© Bonnie Nance

6 *Foot warmer*

7

Shoulder warmer

8

Hug for the asking

9 *Patient*

10 Conversation piece

Pocket pal

© Sharon Eide / Elizabeth Flynn

12 *Lap-top*

13 *Fellow traveler*

14 *Seat saver*

15 *Someone to study with …*

16 *...or play hooky with*

17

Someone to lift your spirits . . .

18 *and share your hobbies*

19 Cargo

© Bonnie Nance

20 *Hide-and-seek partner*

21

Someone to share your lunch…

© Norvia Behling

22 *and your crayons*

24 Dream catchers

© Norvia Behling

26 *Gossip*

Someone to brave the slopes with

28 *Portable heater*

29 *Doll*

© Bonnie Nance

30 *First mate*

31 *Someone to grow up with . . .*

© Norvia Bahling

32 *. . . and grow old with*

. . . helping around the house

33 *Bookend*

© Ron Kimball Studios

35 *Bakery supervisor*

© Norvia Behling

36 *Sous-chef*

37

Help fold the laundry . . .

. . . or carve a jack-o-lantern

© Nancy McCallum

39 Refinish your furniture

© Norvia Behling

40 *Give your boots an authentic,*
well-worn look

Window treatment

© Norvia Behling

42 *Fabric softener*

Plant fertilizer

44 *Private eye*

Help with planting

46 Scare off pests

47 Gatekeeper

© Ron Kimball Studios

Solar heat cell

© Nervia Behling

49 *Christmas tree trimmer*

50 *Christmas ornament*

© Sharon Eide / Elizabeth Flynn

53 *Handyman's helper*

© Sharon Eide / Elizabeth Flynn

54 *Roto-Rooter*

© Bonnie Nance

55 Child nutrition consultants

© Richard Hamilton Smith

56 *Troublemaker*

© Sharon Eide / Elizabeth Flynn

58 Butlers

© Bonnie Nance

60 Groundskeeper

Seat warmers

62 *Pillow*

Odor eaters

© Alan & Sandy Carey

Fur hat

65 Six-pack

© Ron Kimball Studios

66 *Lucky charm*

Email correspondent

68 Desk accessory

© Ron Kimball Studios

69 Centerpiece

70 Bookmark

© Ron Kimball Studios

and filling
special
roles

Choose a fine wine

© PlaceStock Photo.com

72

Pick up chicks

73 Street performer

© Sally Weigand

High-wire walker

76 Acrobat

77 *Snow angel*

78 *Prima donna*

80 *Femme fatale*

© Sharon Eide / Elizabeth Flynn

82 Car alarm

Bumper sticker

© Carol Simowitz

84 *Hood ornament*

85 *Pandora's box*

© Sharon Eide / Elizabeth Flynn

87 *Furball*

88 Goofball

90 *Clowns*

Teddy bear

92 Dog

© Bonnie Nance

96 Poet

97 *Pianist*

98 *Librarians*

© Cheryl A. Ertelt

Best friend